C.G.D Roberts

New York Nocturnes

And Other Poems

C.G.D Roberts

New York Nocturnes
And Other Poems

ISBN/EAN: 9783744713955

Printed in Europe, USA, Canada, Australia, Japan

Cover: Foto ©Thomas Meinert / pixelio.de

More available books at **www.hansebooks.com**

New York Nocturnes

And Other Poems

By

Charles G. D. Roberts

VT CRESCIT

Lamson, Wolffe and Company
Boston, New York and London
MDCCCXCVIII

THE IDEAL

To Her, when life was little worth,
  When hope, a tide run low,
Between dim shores of emptiness
  Almost forgot to flow, —

Faint with the city's fume and stress
  I came at night to Her.
Her cool white fingers on my face —
  How wonderful they were!

More dear they were to fevered lids
  Than lilies cooled in dew.
They touched my lips with tenderness,
  Till life was born anew.

The city's clamour died in calm;
  And once again I heard
The moon-white woodland stillnesses
  Enchanted by a bird;

The wash of far, remembered waves;
  The sigh of lapsing streams;
And one old garden's lilac leaves
  Conferring in their dreams.

A breath from childhood daisy fields
  Came back to me again,
Here in the city's weary miles
  Of city-wearied men.

CONTENTS

NEW YORK NOCTURNES

Contents

New York Nocturnes

'Ω Θεοί, τίς ἄρα Κύπρις, ἢ τίς ἵμερος, τοῦδε

New York Nocturnes

In the Crowd

I walk the city square with thee.
  The night is loud; the pavements roar.
Their eddying mirth and misery
Encircle thee and me.

The street is full of lights and cries.
  The crowd but brings thee close to me.
I only hear thy low replies;
I only see thine eyes.

Night in a Down-town Street

Not in the eyed, expectant gloom,
  Where soaring peaks repose
And incommunicable space
  Companions with the snows;

Not in the glimmering dusk that crawls
  Upon the clouded sea,
Where bourneless wave on bourneless wave
  Complains continually;

Night in a Down-town Street

Not in the palpable dark of woods
　Where groping hands clutch fear,
Does Night her deeps of solitude
　Reveal unveiled as here.

The street is a grim cañon carved
　In the eternal stone,
That knows no more the rushing stream
　It anciently has known.

The emptying tide of life has drained
　The iron channel dry.
Strange winds from the forgotten day
　Draw down, and dream, and sigh.

New York Nocturnes and Other Poems

The narrow heaven, the desolate moon
   Made wan with endless years,
Seem less immeasurably remote
   Than laughter, love, or tears.

At the Railway Station

Here the night is fierce with light,
  Here the great wheels come and go,
Here are partings, waitings, meetings,
  Mysteries of joy and woe.

Here is endless haste and change,
  Here the ache of streaming eyes,
Radiance of expectant faces,
  Breathless askings, brief replies.

Here the jarred, tumultuous air
  Throbs and pauses like a bell,
Gladdens with delight of greeting,
  Sighs and sorrows with farewell.

Here, ah, here with hungry eyes
  I explore the passing throng.
Restless I await your coming
  Whose least absence is so long.

Faces, faces pass me by,
  Meaningless, and blank, and dumb,
Till my heart grows faint and sickens
  Lest at last you should not come.

At the Railway Station

Then — I see you.   And the blood
  Surges back to heart and brain.
Eyes meet mine, — and Heaven opens.
  You are at my side again.

Nocturnes of the Honeysuckle

I

Forever shed your sweetness on the night,
Dear honeysuckle, flower of our delight!

Forever breathe the mystery of that hour
When her hand touched me, lightlier than a
  flower,—

And life became forever strange and sweet, ·
A gift to lay with worship at her feet.

II

Oh, flower of the honeysuckle,
  Tell me how often the long night through
She turns in her dream to the open window,
  She turns in her dream to you.

Oh, flower of the honeysuckle,
  Tell me how tenderly out of the dew
You breathe her a dream of that night of wonder
  When life was fashioned anew.

Oh, flower of the honeysuckle,
  Tell me how long ere, the sweet night through,
She will turn not to you but to me in the darkness,
  And dream and desire come true.

My Garden

I have a garden in the city's grime
Where secretly my heart keeps summer time;

Where blow such airs of rapture on my eyes
As those blest dreamers know in Paradise,

Who after lives of longing come at last
Where anguish of vain love is overpast.

When the broad noon lies shadeless on the street,
And traffic roars, and toilers faint with heat,

Where men forget that ever woods were green,
The wonders of my garden are not seen.

My Garden

Only at night the magic doors disclose
Its labyrinths of lavender and rose;

And honeysuckle, white beneath its moon,
Whispers me softly thou art coming soon;

And led by Love's white hand upon my wrist
Beside its glimmering fountains I keep tryst.

O Love, this moving fragrance on my hair, —
Is it thy breath, or some enchanted air

From far, uncharted realms of mystery
Which I have dreamed of but shall never see?

O Love, this low, wild music in my ears,
Is it the heart-beat of thy hopes and fears,

New York Nocturnes and Other Poems

Or the faint cadence of some fairy song
On winds of boyhood memory blown along?

O Love, what poignant ecstasy is this
Upon my lips and eyes? Thy touch, — thy kiss.

Presence

Dawn like a lily lies upon the land
Since I have known the whiteness of your hand.
Dusk is more soft and more mysterious where
Breathes on my eyes the perfume of your hair.
Waves at your coming break in livelier blue;
And solemn woods are glad because of you.
Brooks of your laughter learn their liquid notes.
Birds to your voice attune their pleading throats.
Fields to your feet grow smoother and more green;
And happy blossoms tell where you have been.

Twilight on Sixth Avenue

Over the tops of the houses
    Twilight and sunset meet.
The green, diaphanous dusk
    Sinks to the eager street.

Astray in the tangle of roofs
    Wanders a wind of June.
The dial shines in the clock-tower
    Like the face of a strange-scrawled moon.

Twilight on Sixth Avenue

The narrowing lines of the houses
  Palely begin to gleam,
And the hurrying crowds fade softly
  Like an army in a dream.

Above the vanishing faces
  A phantom train flares on
With a voice that shakes the shadows,—
  Diminishes, and is gone.

And I walk with the journeying throng
  In such a solitude
As where a lonely ocean
  Washes a lonely wood.

The Street Lamps

Eyes of the city,
Keeping your sleepless watch from sun to sun,
Is it for pity
You tremble, seeing innocence undone;
Or do you laugh, to think men thus should set
Spies on the folly day would fain forget?

24

In Darkness

I have faced life with courage,— but not now!
O Infinite, in this darkness draw thou near.
Wisdom alone I asked of thee, but thou
Hast crushed me with the awful gift of fear.

In the Solitude of the City

Night; and the sound of voices in the street.
Night; and the happy laûghter where they meet,
  The glad boy lover and the trysting girl.
But thou — but thou — I cannot find thee, Sweet!

Night; and far off the lighted pavements roar.
Night; and the dark of sorrow keeps my door.
  I reach my hand out trembling in the dark.
Thy hand comes not with comfort any more.

In the Solitude of the City

O Silent, Unresponding! If these fears
Lie not, nor other wisdom come with years,
  No day shall dawn for me without regret,
No night go uncompanioned by my tears.

A Nocturne of Exile

Out of this night of lonely noise,
  The city's crowded cries,
Home of my heart, to thee, to thee
  I turn my longing eyes.

Years, years, how many years I went
  In exile wearily,
Before I lifted up my face
  And saw my home in thee.

A Nocturne of Exile

I had come home to thee at last.
  I saw thy warm lights gleam.
I entered thine abiding joy,—
  Oh, was it but a dream?

Ere I could reckon with my heart
  The sum of our delight,
I was an exile once again
  Here in the hasting night.

Thy doors were shut; thy lights were gone
  From my remembering eyes. —
Only the city's endless throng!
  Only the crowded cries!

A Street Vigil

Here is the street
Made holy by the passing of her feet,—
    The little, tender feet, more sweet than myrrh,
    Which I have washed with tears for love of her.

Here she has gone
Until the very stones have taken on
    A glory from her passing, and the place
    Is tremulous with memory of her face.

A Street Vigil

Here is the room
That holds the light to lighten all my gloom.
 Beyond that blank white window she is sleeping
 Who hath my hope, my health, my fame, in keep-
  ing.

A little peace
Here for a little, ere my vigil cease
 And I turn homeward, shaken with the strife
 Of hope that struggles hopeless, sick for life.

Surely the power
That lifted me from darkness that one hour
 To a dear heaven whereof no word can tell
 Not wantonly will thrust me back to hell.

A Nocturne of Trysting

Broods the hid glory in its sheath of gloom
Till strikes the destined hour, and bursts the
    bloom,
A rapture of white passion and perfume.

    So the long day is like a bud
      That aches with coming bliss,
    Till flowers in light the wondrous night
      That brings me to thy kiss.

A Nocturne of Trysting

Then, with a thousand sorrows forgotten in one
    hour,
  In thy pure eyes and at thy feet I find at last
    my goal;
And life and hope and joy seem but a faint pre-
    vision
  Of the flower that is thy body and the flame
    that is thy soul.

In a City Room

O city night of noises and alarms,
  Your lights may flare, your cables clang and
    rush,
But in the sanctuary of my love's arms
  Your blinding tumult dies into a hush.

My doors are surged about with your unrest;
  Your plangent cares assail my realm of peace;
But when I come unto her quiet breast
  How suddenly your jar and clamor cease!

In a City Room

Then even remembrance of your strifes and pains
　Diminishes to a ghost of sorrows gone,
Remoter than a dream of last year's rains
　Gusty against my window in the dawn.

A Nocturne of Consecration

I talked about you, Dear, the other night,
Having myself alone with my delight.
Alone with dreams and memories of you,
All the divine-houred summer stillness through
I talked of life, of love the always new,
Of tears, and joy,—yet only talked of you.

To the sweet air
That breathed upon my face
The spirit of lilies in a leafy place,
Your breath's caress, the lingering of your hair,
I said—"In all your wandering through the dusk,

A Nocturne of Consecration

Your waitings on the marriages of flowers
Through the long, intimate hours
When soul and sense, desire and love confer,
You must have known the best that God has made.
What do you know of Her?"

Said the sweet air —
"Since I have touched her lips,
Bringing the consecration of her kiss,
Half passion and half prayer,
And all for you,
My various lore has suffered an eclipse.
I have forgot all else of sweet I knew."

To the wise earth,
Kind, and companionable, and dewy cool,

Fair beyond words to tell, as you are fair,
And cunning past compare
To leash all heaven in a windless pool,
I said — "The mysteries of death and birth
Are in your care.
You love, and sleep; you drain life to the lees;
And wonderful things you know.
Angels have visited you, and at your knees
Learned what I learn forever at her eyes,
The pain that still enhances Paradise.
You in your breast felt her first pulses stir;
And you have thrilled to the light touch of her
    feet,
Blindingly sweet.
Now make me wise with some new word of Her."

A Nocturne of Consecration

Said the wise earth —
"She is not all my child.
But the wild spirit that rules her heart-beats wild
Is of diviner birth
And kin to the unknown light beyond my ken.
All I can give to Her have I not given?
Strength to be glad, to suffer, and to know;
The sorcery that subdues the souls of men;
The beauty that is as the shadow of heaven;
The hunger of love
And unspeakable joy thereof.
And these are dear to Her because of you.
You need no word of mine to make you wise
Who worship at her eyes
And find there life and love forever new!"

To the white stars,
Eternal and all-seeing,
In their wide home beyond the wells of being,
I said — "There is a little cloud that mars
The mystical perfection of her kiss.
Mine, mine, She is,
As far as lip to lip, and heart to heart,
And spirit to spirit when lips and hands must part,
Can make her mine. But there is more than
    this, —
More, more of Her to know.
For still her soul escapes me unaware,
To dwell in secret where I may not go.
Take, and uplift me. Make me wholly Hers."

A Nocturne of Consecration

Said the white stars, the heavenly ministers,—
"This life is brief, but it is only one.
Before to-morrow's sun
For one or both of you it may be done.
This love of yours is only just begun.
Will all the ecstasy that may be won
Before this life its little course has run
At all suffice
The love that agonizes in your eyes?
Therefore be wise.
Content you with the wonder of love that lies
Between her lips and underneath her eyes.
If more you should surprise,
What would be left to hope from Paradise?

In other worlds expect another joy
Of Her, which blundering fate shall not annoy,
Nor time nor change destroy."

So, Dear, I talked the long, divine night through,
And felt you in the chrismal balms of dew.
The thing then learned
Has ever since within my bosom burned —
One life is not enough for love of you.

Other Poems

An Evening Communion

The large first stars come out
  Above the open hill,
And in the west the light
  Is lingering still.

The wide and tranquil air
  Of evening washes cool
On open hill, and vale,
  And shining pool.

The calm of endless time
  Is in the spacious hour,
Whose mystery unfolds
  To perfect flower.

The silence and my heart
  Expect a voice I know,—
A voice we have not heard
  Since long ago.

Since long ago thy face,
  Thy smile, I may not see,
True comrade, whom the veil
  Divides from me.

An Evening Communion

But when earth's hidden word
    I almost understand,
.I dream that on my lips
    I feel thy hand.

Thy presence is the light
    Upon the open hill.
Thou walkest with me here,
    True comrade still.

My pain and my unrest
    Thou tak'st into thy care.
The world becomes a dream,
    And life a prayer.

Life and Art

Said Life to Art — "I love thee best
 Not when I find in thee
My very face and form, expressed
 With dull fidelity,

"But when in thee my craving eyes
 Behold continually
The mystery of my memories
 And all I long to be."

Beyond the Tops of Time

How long it was I did not know,
  That I had waited, watched, and feared.
It seemed a thousand years ago
  The last pale lights had disappeared.
I knew the place was a narrow room
Up, up beyond the reach of doom.

Then came a light more red than flame; —
  No sun-dawn, but the soul laid bare
Of earth and sky and sea became
  A presence burning everywhere;
And I was glad my narrow room
Was high above the reach of doom.

Windows there were in either wall,
  Deep cleft, and set with radiant glass,
Wherethrough I watched the mountains fall,
  The ages wither up and pass.
I knew their doom could never climb
My tower beyond the tops of Time.

A sea of faces then I saw,
  Of men who had been, men long dead.
Figured with dreams of joy and awe
  The heavens unrolled in lambent red;
While far below the faces cried—
"Give us the dream for which we died!"

Beyond the Tops of Time

Ever the woven shapes rolled by
  Above the faces hungering.
With quiet and incurious eye
  I noted many a wondrous thing,—
Seas of clear glass, and singing streams,
In that high pageantry of dreams;

Cities of sard and chrysoprase
  Where choired Hosannas never cease;
Valhallas of celestial frays,
  And lotus-pools of endless peace;
But still the faces gaped and cried —
"Give us the dream for which we died!"

At length my quiet heart was stirred,
  Hearing them cry so long in vain.
But while I listened for a word
  That should translate them from their pain,
I saw that here and there a face
Shone, and was lifted from its place,

And flashed into the moving dome
  An ecstasy of prismed fire.
And then said I, "A soul has come
  To the deep zenith of desire!"
But still I wondered if it knew
The dream for which it died was true.

Beyond the Tops of Time

I wondered — who shall say how long?
  (One heart-beat? — Thrice ten thousand years?)
Till suddenly there was no throng
  Of faces to arraign the spheres,—
No more white faces there to cry
To those great pageants of the sky.

Then quietly I grew aware
  Of one who came with eyes of bliss
And brow of calm and lips of prayer.
  Said I — "How wonderful is this!
Where are the faces once that cried —
'Give us the dream for which we died'?"

The answer fell as soft as sleep,—
  "I am of those who, having cried
So long in that tumultuous deep,
  Have won the dream for which we died."
And then said I—"Which dream was true?
For many were revealed to you!"

He answered—"To the soul made wise
  All true, all beautiful they seem.
But the white peace that fills our eyes
  Outdoes desire, outreaches dream.
For we are come unto the place
Where always we behold God's face!"

Dream-Fellows

Behind the veil that men call sleep
  I came upon a golden land.
A golden light was in the leaves
  And on the amethystine strand.

Amber and gold and emerald
  The unimaginable wood.
And in a joy I could not name
  Beside the emerald stream I stood.

ʼDown from a violet hill came one
　　Running to meet me on the shore.
I clasped his hand.　He seemed to be
　　One I had long been waiting for.

All the sweet sounds I ever heard
　　In his low greeting seemed to blend.
His were the eyes of my true love.
　　His was the mouth of my true friend.

We spoke; and the transfigured words
　　Meant more than words had ever meant.
Our lips at last forgot to speak,
　　For silence was so eloquent.

Dream-Fellows

We floated in the emerald stream;
  We wandered in the wondrous wood.
His soul to me was clear as light.
  My inmost thought he understood.

Only to be was to be glad.
  Life, like a rainbow, filled our eyes.
In comprehending comradeship
  Each moment seemed a Paradise.

And often, in the after years,
  I and my dream-fellow were one
For hours together in that land
  Behind the moon, beyond the sun.

At last, in the tumultuous dream
  That men call life, I chanced to be
One day amid the city throng
  Where the great piers oppose the sea.

A giant ship was swinging off
  For other seas and other skies.
Amid the voyaging companies
  I saw his face, I saw his eyes.

Oh, passionately through the crowd
  I thrust, and then — our glances met!
Across the widening gulf we gazed,
  With white set lips, and eyes grown wet.

Dream-Fellows

And all day long my heart was faint
  With parting pangs and tears unwept;
Till night brought comfort, for he came
  To meet me, smiling, when I slept.

Beyond the veil that men call sleep
  We met, within that golden land.
He said — or I — "We grieved to-day.
  But now, more wise, we understand!

"Communing in the common world,
  The flesh, for us, would be a bar.
Strange would be our familiar speech;
  And earth would seem no more a star.

"We'd know no more the golden leaves
　　Beside the amethystine deep;
We'd see no more each other's thought
　　Behind the veil that men call sleep!"

`

The Atlantic Cable

This giant nerve, at whose command
  The world's great pulses throb or sleep, —
It threads the undiscerned repose
  Of the dark bases of the deep.

Around it settle in the calm
  Fine tissues that a breath might mar,
Nor dream what fiery tidings pass,
  What messages of storm and war.

Far over it, where filtered gleams
  Faintly illume the mid-sea day,
Strange, pallid forms of fish or weed
  In the obscure tide softly sway.

And higher, where the vagrant waves
  Frequent the white, indifferent sun,
Where ride the smoke-blue hordes of rain
  And the long vapors lift and run,

Passes perhaps some lonely ship
  With exile hearts that homeward ache,—
While far beneath is flashed a word
  That soon shall bid them bleed or break.

When the Clover blooms again

"When the clover blooms again,
And the rain-birds in the rain
  Make the sad-heart noon seem sweeter
  And the joy of June completer
I shall see his face again!"

Of her lover over sea
So she whispered happily;
  And she prayed, while men were sleeping,
  "Mary, have him in thy keeping
As he sails the stormy sea!"

White and silent lay his face
In a still, green-watered place,
  Where the long, gray weed scarce lifted,
  And the sand was lightly sifted
O'er his unremembering face.

At Tide Water

The red and yellow of the Autumn salt-grass,
  The gray flats, and the yellow-gray full tide,
The lonely stacks, the grave expanse of marshes,—
  O Land wherein my memories abide,
I have come back that you may make me tranquil,
  Resting a little at your heart of peace,
Remembering much amid your serious leisure,
  Forgetting more amid your large release.
For yours the wisdom of the night and morning,
  The word of the inevitable years,
The open Heaven's unobscured communion,
  And the dim whisper of the wheeling spheres.

New York Nocturnes and Other Poems

The great things and the terrible I bring you,
  To be illumined in your spacious breath,—
Love, and the ashes of desire, and anguish,
  Strange laughter, and the unhealing wound of
    death.
These in the world, all these, have come upon me,
  Leaving me mute and shaken with surprise.
Oh, turn them in your measureless contemplation,
  And in their mastery teach me to be wise.

The Falling Leaves

Lightly He blows, and at His breath they fall,
  The perishing kindreds of the leaves; they drift,
Spent flames of scarlet, gold aerial,
  Across the hollow year, noiseless and swift.
Lightly He blows, and countless as the falling
  Of snow by night upon a solemn sea,
The ages circle down beyond recalling,
  To strew the hollows of Eternity.
He sees them drifting through the spaces dim,
  And leaves and ages are as one to Him.

Marjory

(A Backwoods Ballad)

Spring, summer, autumn, winter,
　Over the wild world rolls the year.
Comes June to the rose-red tamarack buds,
　But Marjory comes not here.

The pastures miss her; the house without her
　Grows forgotten, and gray, and old;
The wind, and the lonely light of the sun,
　Are heavy with tears untold.

Marjory

Spring, summer, autumn, winter,
  Morning, evening, over and o'er!
The swallow returns to the nested rafter,
  But Marjory comes no more.

The gray barn-doors in the long wind rattle
  Hour by hour of the long white day.
The horses fret by the well-filled manger
  Since Marjory went away.

The sheep she fed at the bars await her.
  The milch cows low for her down the lane.
They long for her light, light hand at the milk-
      ing,—
  They long for her hand in vain.

Spring, summer, autumn, winter,
  Morning and evening, over and o'er!
The bees come back with the willow catkins,
  But Marjory comes no more.

The voice of the far-off city called to her.
  Was it long years or an hour ago?
She went away, with dear eyes weeping,
  To a world she did not know.

The berried pastures they could not keep her,
  The brook, nor the buttercup-golden hill,
Nor even the long, long love familiar,—
  The strange voice called her still.

Marjory

She would not stay for the old home garden; —
    The scarlet poppy, the mignonette,
The fox-glove bell, and the kind-eyed pansy,
    Their hearts will not forget.

Oh, that her feet had not forgotten
    The woodland country, the homeward way!
Oh, to look out of the sad, bright window
    And see her come back, some day!

Spring, summer, autumn, winter,
    Over the wild world rolls the year.
Comes joy to the bird on the nested rafter;
    But Marjory comes not here.

The Solitary Woodsman

When the gray lake-water rushes
Past the dripping alder bushes,
  And the bodeful autumn wind
In the fir-tree weeps and hushes,—

When the air is sharply damp
Round the solitary camp,
  And the moose-bush in the thicket
Glimmers like a scarlet lamp,—

The Solitary Woodsman

When the birches twinkle yellow,
And the cornel bunches mellow,
  And the owl across the twilight
Trumpets to his downy fellow,—

When the nut-fed chipmunks romp
Through the maples' crimson pomp,
  And the slim viburnum flushes
In the darkness of the swamp,—

When the blueberries are dead,
When the rowan clusters red,
  And the shy bear, summer-sleekened,
In the bracken makes his bed,—

On a day there comes once more
To the latched and lonely door,
  Down the wood-road striding silent,
One who has been here before.

Green spruce branches for his head,
Here he makes his simple bed,
  Couching with the sun, and rising
When the dawn is frosty red.

All day long he wanders wide
With the gray moss for his guide,
  And his lonely axe-stroke startles
The expectant forest-side.

The Solitary Woodsman

Toward the quiet close of day
Back to camp he takes his way,
　And about his sober footsteps
Unafraid the squirrels play.

On his roof the red leaf falls,
At his door the blue-jay calls,
　And he hears the wood-mice hurry
Up and down his rough log walls;

Hears the laughter of the loon
Thrill the dying afternoon,—
　Hears the calling of the moose
Echo to the early moon.

And he hears the partridge drumming,
The belated hornet humming,—
    All the faint, prophetic sounds
That foretell the winter's coming.

And the wind about his eaves
Through the chilly night-wet grieves,
    And the earth's dumb patience fills him,
Fellow to the falling leaves.

The Stirrup Cup

Life at my stirrup lifted wistful eyes,
  And as she gave the parting cup to me,—
  Death's pale companion for the silent sea,—
"I know," she said, "that land and where it lies.
  A pledge between us now before you go,
  That when you meet me there your soul may
    know!"

Ice

When Winter scourged the meadow and the hill
And in the withered leafage worked his will,
The water shrank, and shuddered, and stood still,—
Then built himself a magic house of glass,   .
Irised with memories of flowers and grass,
Wherein to sit and watch the fury pass.

The Hermit

Above the blindness of content,
  The ignorance of ease,
Inhabiting within his soul
  A shrine of memories,

Between the silences of sleep
  Attentively he hears
The endless crawling sob and strain,
  The spending of the years.

He sees the lapsing stream go by
    His unperturbed face,
Out of a dark, into a dark,
    Across a lighted space.

He calls it Life, this lighted space
    Upon the moving flood.
He sees the water white with tears,
    He sees it red with blood.

And many specks upon the tide
    He sees and marks by name,—
Motes of a day, and fools of Fate,
    And challengers of fame;

The Hermit

With here a people, there a babe,
  A blossom, or a crown,—
They whirl a little, gleam, and pass,
  Or in the eddies drown.

He waits. He waits one day to see
  The lapsing of the stream,
The eddying forms, the darknesses,
  Dissolve into a dream.

"O Thou who bidd'st"

O Thou who bidd'st a million germs decay
That one white bloom may soar into the day,
Mine eyes unseal to see their souls in death
Borne back to Thee upon the lily's breath.

Ascription

O Thou who hast beneath Thy hand
The dark foundations of the land,—
The motion of whose ordered thought
An instant universe hath wrought,—

Who hast within Thine equal heed
The rolling sun, the ripening seed,
The azure of the speedwell's eye,
The vast solemnities of sky,—

Who hear'st no less the feeble note
Of one small bird's awakening throat,
Than that unnamed, tremendous chord
Arcturus sounds before his Lord,—

More sweet to Thee than all acclaim
Of storm and ocean, stars and flame,
In favour more before Thy face
Than pageantry of time and space,

The worship and the service be
Of him Thou madest most like Thee,—
Who in his nostrils hath Thy breath,
Whose spirit is the lord of death!

*Set up by J. S. Cushing & Co., and printed by Berwick & Smith, at the Norwood Press, for the publishers, Lamson, Wolffe & Co., in the year Eighteen Hundred and Ninety-eight. * * **

www.ingramcontent.com/pod-product-compliance
Lightning Source LLC
Chambersburg PA
CBHW031454270326
41930CB00007B/1000